THE NEW PLANT LIBRARY

SUMMER BULBS

THE NEW PLANT LIBRARY

SUMMER BULBS

P E T E R M C H O Y

Photography by Peter Anderson

LORENZ BOOKS

First published in 1998 by Lorenz Books

© Anness Publishing Limited 1998

Lorenz Books is an imprint of
Anness Publishing Limited
Hermes House
88-89 Blackfriars Road
London SE1 8HA

This edition published in the USA by Lorenz Books, Anness Publishing Inc.,
27 West 20th Street, New York, NY 10011; (800) 354 9657

This edition distributed in Canada by Raincoast Books
8680 Cambie Street, Vancouver, British Columbia, V6P 6M9

ISBN 1 85967 636 7

A CIP catalogue record for this book is available
from the British Library

Publisher Joanna Lorenz
Editor Margaret Malone
Designer Julie Francis
Photographer Peter Anderson

Printed in Hong Kong/China

1 3 5 7 9 10 8 6 4 2

■ HALF TITLE PAGE
Gladiolus, butterfly
■ FRONTISPIECE
Cannas in mixed border
■ TITLE PAGE
Lilium, Asiatic hybrid

■ THIS PAGE
Dahlia 'Bishop of Llandaff'
■ OPPOSITE LEFT
Dahlia, miniature ball
■ OPPOSITE RIGHT
Liatris spicata

Contents

Introduction

Mention the word bulbs, and most people think of spring-flowering plants. But summer, and indeed autumn bulbs, are just as exciting.

The majestic summer lilies come in a multitude of colours as well as many different shapes and sizes, and gladioli can have as much bold impact as any bed of summer roses. And for the discerning gardener, there are gems like the pineapple lily (*Eucomis bicolor*) and the blood lily (*Haemanthus*).

If you have a conservatory or greenhouse there are even exotics like the climbing lily (*Gloriosa superba*), or the fragrant tuberose (*Polianthes tuberosa*), while frost-tender bulbs like the velvet-trumpeted gloxinias (*Sinningia speciosa*) and long-flowering hot water plants (*Achimenes*) make splendid houseplants. The choice is huge and varied.

■ RIGHT
Ranunculus asiaticus are often bought as tubers, but 'Accolade', shown here, can be raised from seed.

What is a bulb?

Many of the bulbs mentioned in this book are not true bulbs at all. Plants that grow from corms, tubers, and rhizomes are also included because they are often collectively referred to as bulbs. You can buy the plants mentioned from bulb merchants or bulb specialists, although a few are also sold as growing plants or in pots.

The majority of bulbs are dormant storage organs that can be lifted from the ground and sold dry, although a few transplant best if lifted in the green, i.e. still with leaves. A few of the plants included, such as agapanthus, which have fleshy roots, and *Hemerocallis* (day lilies), with their rhizomatous roots, are often thought of as ordinary herbaceous plants and are usually bought pot-grown. As they qualify on technical grounds, however, we have included them here.

Spring into summer

This book includes only bulbs that have their main flowering period from early summer to late autumn, but defining the flowering period exactly is not, in fact, that easy. Those that flower in late spring may continue into early summer. And in a cold area or a late season, these plants may have an even longer period of flower in early summer than they would in late spring.

Some excellent border bulbs fall into this category, including many alliums (ornamental onions) and camassias, and can easily be overlooked.

An anemone tuber.

Botanical characteristics

A true bulb resembles an onion, with distinct layers or scales clearly visible if it is cut in half. Usually these are encased in an outer papery skin, but in lilies the individual scales may be separate and more clearly exposed.

A corm is similar in shape, normally with a symmetrical outline, but the flesh is solid when cut and not composed of scales. Tubers are usually more irregular in shape, with more than one "eye" or growth bud (not always clearly visible), and they also lack the distinctive layers or scales visible in bulbs.

Rhizomes are underground stems that grow horizontally below or close to the surface of the soil.

Roots grow from the bottom of the rhizome, with leaves from the side or top.

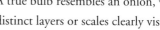

A galtonia bulb.

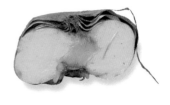

A gladiolus corm.

■ RIGHT
■ RIGHT
The large bright dahlias are popular cut flowers, widely used in floral art. They also make pleasing plants for a border.

■ BELOW
Crocosmias are ideal plants for herbaceous borders, making large clumps that shout their presence when in bloom.

Be bold with bulbs

Summer and autumn bulbs are seldom used in large drifts, or with other bedding plants, as are spring bulbs. The majority of them are best treated like ordinary plants in herbaceous or mixed borders, or perhaps used to add foreground interest and colour in a shrub border. Some are at home in the rock garden, while others make pleasing container plants. Lilies, for example, are multi-purpose, being ideal for the edge of a woodland area, for bringing colour to a planting of shrubs, and for growing in containers. A few bulbs, such as dahlias, can even be used to create a bold, brash effect when a whole border is planted with them.

Cutting for the home

Bulbs provide some outstanding summer cut flowers. There is a large cut-flower trade in gladioli, for example, which in many ways are more successful cut and used in arrangements than in herbaceous or mixed borders. Dutch irises are also more often seen as cut flowers than as garden plants, even though they make a pleasing – albeit brief – display in the garden.

Border beauty

Those plants hardy enough to be left to grow and multiply in a herbaceous or mixed border will often make large and imposing clumps. Crocosmias, for example, multiply freely and soon make large clumps of glowing orange or red flowers that can become a focal point, taking the eye across the garden.

A touch of the tropical

Cannas, with their tall spikes of orange, red, pink or yellow flowers, are often used for sub-tropical bedding in public parks, but they will add a touch of the exotic planted towards the back of a herbaceous border. You could also try planting a drift of caladiums (*Caladium bicolor* hybrids) with their almost paper-thin, heart-shaped leaves variegated pink, red, green and white.

One of the most exotic plants that you can grow is the climbing lily (*Gloriosa superba*). It has strongly reflexed petals that combine yellow and red in a way that resembles a dancing flame.

The world of bulbs

■ LEFT
Zantedeschias will thrive outdoors in mild areas, yet perish in cold ones. They will grow in shallow water or on land, make an attractive pot plant for a greenhouse, and are sold widely as cut flowers. How you use such plants depends on where you garden, and what protection you can offer.

These packages of pent-up beauty waiting to be released that we call bulbs show immense diversity, and are suitable for many different climates and soil types. Some like to be baked in hot sun, others need moist soil or woodland shade. Although they are grown commercially on a large scale in relatively few countries, such as Holland, the USA and South Africa, they are native to many different parts of the world. Many of the summer and autumn flowering bulbs are fortunately frost-hardy, but some are tender and should be given winter protection.

Understanding the conditions that summer bulbs require is important to a successful display. Autumn bulbs, like spring ones, are generally hardy and tolerant of a wide range of conditions. The summer-flowering bulbs, however, are often more temperamental and demand a more in-depth knowledge of their requirements. Many of them grow naturally in South Africa, tigridias and *Polianthes tuberosa* come from Mexico among other places, caladiums from tropical South America, and gloriosas from Africa. These are very diverse climates, and temperatures, soils, rainfall and humidity may be vastly different to what they will receive in your garden.

In relatively warm climates such as California, the majority of bulbs mentioned in this book can be grown outdoors all the year round, but in cooler climates some will require lifting for winter protection. A few are best grown permanently in pots in a greenhouse or conservatory, though they can also be used as short-term house plants.

Signs of good breeding

Breeders have changed many popular bulbs to pinnacles of perfection far removed from the species from which they derive. Nowadays, we do not grow in our gardens true species of dahlias, for example, but use instead

■ RIGHT
Lilies are extensively hybridized, producing a wonderful array of beautiful blooms from which to choose. This one is 'Cover Girl'.

the hybrids that have been developed by generations of gardeners and breeders. Most of the gladioli that we grow are the result of the hybridist's skills, and although many true species of lilies are grown it is the hybrids that have helped to make them so popular.

There are specialist societies for enthusiasts of plants such as dahlias, gladioli, and lilies. Dahlias are often grown as exhibition blooms, and show classes are held for gladioli and lilies too. New varieties are

constantly being developed, and as they come on the market old inferior ones drop out of commercial production. And with so many varieties, those available in one country may not be sold in another, which means that not all the varieties illustrated in this book will be universally available . . . but you are sure to be able to buy similar or even better varieties.

■ LEFT
Modern dahlias are far removed from the species from which they derive, and new varieties are being introduced every year. Once, the only fully double varieties were tall plants best in a border, nowadays there are dwarfs for patio pots.

Looking natural

Naturalized bulbs – those planted in grass or perhaps in the ground beneath trees or shrubs – are ideal if you are looking for a no-fuss, trouble-free way to grow your bulbs and multiply your investment at the same time. Those suitable for naturalizing usually multiply over the years and look better year-by-year. They only require lifting and dividing if they become so overcrowded that flowering begins to suffer.

Spring-flowering bulbs such as crocuses and daffodils are the most usual choice, but autumn-flowering

■ ABOVE
Dwarf hardy cyclamen, such as *C. hederifolium*, here flowering in early autumn, are robust enough to flower well beneath the canopy of large trees.

■ LEFT
Colchicums are ideal for naturalizing beneath shrubs or small trees. *C. speciosum* 'Album' shows up particularly well in a shady position.

■ RIGHT
True crocuses that flower in the autumn, such as *C. nudiflorus,* make a pleasing show in short grass.

true crocuses, such as *C. speciosus,* and the so-called autumn crocuses that are actually colchicums, look wonderful planted in short grass, in drifts beneath trees, or in front of shrubs. The autumn-flowering miniature cyclamen can make a fantastic sight carpeting the ground beneath a large tree. *Cyclamen hederifolium* (syn. *C. neapolitanum*) is the best-known species, starting to bloom in late summer and continuing until early or mid-autumn. The corms can eventually be 30cm (12in) across, so do not plant them too closely.

Fewer summer-flowering bulbs are suitable for this treatment, but try the reddish-purple *Gladiolus communis* ssp. *byzantinus* in an orchard, or where the grass is more meadow-like, as the flower stems reach about 75cm (2½ft). *Brodiaea laxa* (now more correctly called *Triteleia laxa*), with its loose heads of blue flowers on wiry stems about 30–45cm (1–1½ft) tall, also naturalizes well where the grass is not too tall.

Even lilies can be naturalized in open woodland or even in an open grassed area, but you need to choose both the lily and the grass with care. The lily species rather than the hybrids naturalize most readily.

Suitable species include *L. hansonii, L. martagon,* and *L. pardalinum,* the last preferring damp soil.

Watch that grass

Tall, unkempt grass, perhaps in a neglected area, is not a good place in which to naturalize summer or autumn bulbs. They are unlikely to compete with the grass, even if you can see them above it. The grass needs to be mown once or twice a year when the bulbs are dormant. Better still, plant the bulbs then sow the grass, choosing fine fescues. That way they will both become established without too much competition, and the bulbs will not be submerged by taller and more rampant grasses.

SAVING MONEY

You need a large number of bulbs for naturalizing, even in a small garden, as they need to be planted in a large drift to look effective. This can make the initial investment costly if you have to buy them as bulbs, corms or tubers. Fortunately many of those plants that are best for naturalizing, such as *Crocus speciosus* and *Cyclamen hederifolium,* are easily raised from seed.

Be prepared to wait for an extra year or two for results, but raising your own plants from seed can be a cost-effective means of providing a large number of plants for this purpose.

Beds and borders

Summer-flowering bulbs are exceptionally good for adding highlights to a traditional herbaceous border, and can work magic among shrubs whose display has already finished. As the bulbs die back in the autumn they are unobtrusive, yet they emerge from among the foliage cover of other plants the following year to burst upon the world with a stunning display of brilliance as their blooms open.

Growing among shrubs

Lilies are the first choice for a border containing mainly shrubs, especially dwarf shrubs such as hebes, dwarf rhododendrons and Christmas box (*Sarcococca* species).

The Christmas box is an example of a shrub that earns its keep in winter when its small, inconspicuous flowers fill the air with a heady fragrance on a cold winter's day. Lily bulbs planted behind will emerge for their moment of summer glory, and the dwarf box in front will enhance the display by hiding the rather leggy appearance of the lily stems. The lilies later die back or are cut back to allow the shrub its own moment of glory.

If the shrubs grow larger than the bulbs you intend to plant, clear a space in front of the shrubs. Dark green shrub foliage makes an excellent backdrop against which to view, for example, the magnificent white trumpets of *Lilium regale*, or perhaps a clump of the white-flowered summer hyacinth, *Galtonia candicans*.

Herbaceous and mixed borders

There is always room for at least a couple of clumps of lilies as they tend to grow upwards rather than outwards, and can almost grow through more spreading herbaceous plants. But the choice of bulbs is much wider, and it is difficult to imagine a traditional herbaceous border without a clump or two of crocosmias. The corms multiply freely, and after a year or two most plantings make a bold show in late summer with their arching sprays of red, orange or yellow flowers.

Alliums come in many forms, but most of them belong in the herbaceous or mixed border.

■ LEFT
A clump of lilies flowering against a backdrop of dark green shrub foliage can bring a border to life in summer, especially if the shrubs are mainly spring-flowering.

■ LEFT
Crocosmias and dwarf dahlias make a bold contribution to any herbaceous or shrub border.

The choice includes dwarf ones like the yellow *A. moly* and *A. christophii* (syn. *A. albopilosum*), with its 15cm (6in) spheres of starry lilac flowers, planted at the front, with tall majestic species such as the 1.8m (6ft) *A. giganteum* with its huge balls of lilac flowers at the back. *Allium sphaerocephalon*, with its drumstick heads of pinkish-purple flowers on thin and frail-looking stems about 75cm (2½ft) tall, is typical of the alliums best grown mid-border, with other border plants helping to hide and support the stems.

■ BELOW

Allium schubertii grows best in full sun at the front of a border, producing attractive large heads of star-shaped flowers in early summer.

CUTTING A DASH

● Summer bulbs give us some of our most valued cut flowers, such as gladioli, irises and lilies. But you could also try some of the less commonly grown cut flowers, such as *Ornithogalum thyrsoides*, best known as chincherinchee, which produces short, conical spikes of white flowers that will last for up to three weeks indoors.

● If growing lilies for cutting, and you find pollen stains a problem, there are now varieties without pollen – 'Aphrodite' (pink) and 'Sphinx' (orange-red) are two of them.

● It may be possible to provide a supply of cut flowers by taking a few blooms from clumps in the border, but if a lot of cut flowers are required it is best to grow them in a dedicated area set aside for the purpose. Do not be afraid to plant them a little more closely than usual to maximize the number of blooms. Since most of them will be cut as the first buds are opening it is not necessary to consider whether they will look cramped. Bear in mind, however, that close planting may increase the risks of pest or disease problems.

Colour in containers

Tender plants such as tuberous begonias are the commonest choice for summer containers, but with a little imagination many other kinds can be used very effectively.

Unfortunately, most of the summer bulbs have a very short flowering season in comparison with the traditional bedding plants with which they compete; many bloom for weeks rather than months. There are exceptions, of course, and they redeem what would otherwise be a shortcoming among the plants that we loosely call bulbs. None of them are true bulbs, but from a gardening viewpoint it is irrelevant whether they have bulbs or tubers.

Dahlias

These bright, beautiful plants need special mention. This is partly because appropriate varieties make excellent container plants, whether in tubs, troughs or windowboxes, and also because there are still gardeners unaware of modern dwarf varieties; they still think of dahlias as tall, late-flowering plants.

The compact varieties suitable for containers are usually blooming by midsummer, and they will continue until the first frost if deadheaded and fed regularly – a regime that applies to most summer bedding plants, not just dahlias.

Look for varieties described as Patio or Lilliput dahlias, but check the height. Some are very compact, growing to about 30cm (1ft), and are suitable for windowboxes. Others may grow to about 45cm (1½ft), and are more suitable for large patio pots. The dahlias will look better if grown on their own.

Do not be confused by seed-raised bedding dahlias. They can be successful in flower beds but less so as container plants. Instead buy tubers or plants raised from cuttings.

■ ABOVE
Tuberous-rooted bedding begonias provide a long-lasting display in a container, usually blooming until the first frost.

■ LEFT
Bring the outdoors inside by planting up an old trug with autumn-flowering crocus (colchicums) in soil covered in a natural-looking carpet of moss and leaves.

Tubs, troughs, baskets and boxes

Lilies have to be on any short-list of summer bulbs, and they make marvellous container plants. Not so long ago commercial growers dwarfed tall varieties chemically to produce compact plants, but nowadays naturally dwarf varieties are available, with minimal sacrifice of flower size.

Tall varieties, including species such as *Lilium longifolium*, make imposing plants for a focal-point display in a large container, while the more compact varieties that grow to around 30–60cm (1–2ft) are a better choice for a patio.

Bear in mind that since lilies will produce a short-lived display, you need a selection of other bulbs to flower in other pots. A container large enough to take cane supports or a frame can be planted with the climbing lily (*Gloriosa superba*), which is not usually at its best until most of the ordinary lilies are over.

Other bulbs for early or mid-summer that look good in pots include ismenes and cannas. Ismenes have the benefit of fragrance, but the almost daffodil-like flowers are short-lived. Cannas, on the other hand, flower over a long period and the foliage is usually an attractive bronze-red or variegated. For that reason they make a more useful tub plant, though the tall flower stems will require tying to a support if grown in a very exposed position.

Finally, prevent late summer and autumn being a let-down by growing a few bulbs that are at their best when the flush of summer colour begins to wane. Pineapple lilies (*Eucomis* species) and nerines put on a pleasing and long-lasting display in patio pots and containers.

Tuberous begonias are one of the very best bulbs for a summer-long display in a windowbox or basket. There are upright and trailing varieties, both widely available. Dwarf dahlias are another good choice. If fed and deadheaded regularly, they will form an attractive display for a couple of months.

Home and conservatory

If you have a greenhouse or conservatory, be sure to include some of the more tender summer-flowering bulbs, many of which look particularly exotic. Some of them also make pleasing, unusual pot plants to display in the home.

Easy and reliable

Achimenes and sinningias (more usually sold as gloxinias) are readily available, and very easy to grow.

Achimenes are usually available as hybrids, some with a trailing habit suitable for baskets, others with a more upright growth. They bloom over a long period, from early summer to autumn, with flowers mainly in shades of blue, mauve, lavender or pink. Plant three or five of the small cone-like rhizomes to a 20cm (8in) pot.

Sinningias (gloxinias) make superb pot plants and will even succeed on the windowsill if you do not have a greenhouse or conservatory. The bell-shaped flowers can be 10cm (4in) across, and the usually pink, purple or red blooms are often attractively spotted or edged with another colour. Plant a single tuber in a 15cm (6in) pot, with the top of the tuber flush with the surface of the potting soil.

The large-flowered tuberous begonias make pleasing conservatory plants. By removing the female flowers (the small ones behind the main male flowers), and feeding regularly, huge blooms can be easily produced. Those sold as tubers for growing in pots are likely to have bigger blooms than seed-raised ones.

■ LEFT AND ABOVE
Tuberous begonias make pleasing pot plants for a greenhouse or conservatory, and the flowers can be huge.

■ RIGHT
Gloriosa superba is sometimes called the
flame lily. It is easy to see why.

A hint of the exotic

Caladiums have large but paper-thin
leaves, often in rich reds and usually
with contrasting variegation. Since
these plants need a warm, humid
atmosphere to do really well, a
conservatory is better than a living-
room. Start the tubers off in late
winter or spring for best results.

The climbing lily *Gloriosa superba*
is one of those eye-catching plants
that simply demands attention and
admiration. It has wonderful red and
yellow reflexed flowers.

Haemanthus multiflorus (more
correctly called *Scadoxus multiflorus
katherinae*) is sometimes called the
blood lily – not because of its

magnificent globular heads of red
flowers, but because the bulbs are
often covered with red spots.

Sweet fragrance

There are two white-flowered bulbs
with a wonderful fragrance that make
delightful conservatory plants.
Hymenocallis x *festalis* has spidery
looking white and very fragrant
flowers on stems about 60–75cm
(2–2½ft) tall. *Polianthes tuberosa*, the
tuberose, has sweetly scented, white,
waxy flowers that are double
in the variety 'The Pearl'.

FOR A BIT OF FUN

Try flowering a few colchicum
corms in early autumn. They
will bloom even if you do not
plant them, but it is sensible to
stand them in a small container
with some pebbles, to ensure
the large corm and flowers
remain upright. You do not
need to water them, but plant
them in the garden when the
flowers have finished and leaves
will appear in the spring.

■ ABOVE
Caladium bicolor is grown for its highly
decorative leaves, which may be bi- or
tricoloured. It needs warmth and humidity,
but you can dry off the bulbs for winter.

Plant Catalogue

Here is a selection of some of the best summer- and autumn-flowering plants that you can grow from bulbs, corms, tubers or rhizomes, but they can only serve to whet your appetite. There are many more excellent kinds than there is space to illustrate, and a further selection with brief descriptions appears at the end of this book.

■ ABOVE
ACIDANTHERA BICOLOR

A marvellous, late-flowering native of tropical Africa, more correctly named *Gladiolus callianthus*, but usually listed in catalogues as an acidanthera. The flowers resemble a small white gladiolus, with a purple blotch in the centre. The blooms are slightly scented. 'Murielae', shown here, is a slightly larger and more robust plant than the species.

These are especially useful plants because they flower in late summer and early autumn, when most summer flowers are past their best. Height 90cm (3ft). Corm.

■ LEFT
ALLIUM CHRISTOPHII

This native of Iran and other areas of
central Asia is sometimes called star of
Persia. Still sometimes found under its
older name of *A. albopilosum*, it is one of
the most popular of all the ornamental
onions. The large spheres of star-shaped
purple flowers are 15cm (6in) or more
across, and can be dried for winter flower
arrangements. Height 30cm (1ft). Bulb.

■ BELOW
ALLIUM OREOPHILUM

Still sometimes found under its older name of *A. ostrowskianum*,
this native of Turkestan and central Asia spans the period from late
spring to early summer. A small, dainty looking plant, it has
carmine pink flowers that are surprisingly showy despite the plant's
small size. A good choice for the rock garden: it needs good
drainage and plenty of sun to thrive. Height 15cm (6in). Bulb.

■ ABOVE
ALLIUM HYBRIDS

Many of the most spectacular alliums for the herbaceous border are
hybrids with very large drumstick heads. 'Globemaster', which
probably has *A. giganteum* in its ancestry, and 'Globus'
(illustrated), are two fine examples. Both have large heads of rosy-
purple flowers that make a pleasing focal point within the border.
Height 60–150cm (2–5ft). Bulb.

BEGONIA, PENDULOUS

The large-flowered, trailing forms of tuberous begonias are hybrids that derive from several species, as described in the entry for tuberous begonias, but they have a cascading habit that is suitable for hanging baskets or the front of a windowbox. They come in the same colour range as the upright varieties. They may be sold by colour, or be a named variety. The one illustrated is 'Illumination Salmon Pink'. Trailing. Tuber.

BEGONIA, TUBEROUS

The tuberous-rooted begonias used for bedding and summer displays in containers are hybrids derived from many, mainly Andean, species. Sometimes grouped as *B. x tuberhybrida* varieties, they come in shades of pink, red, orange, yellow and white. Most of those sold by bulb companies are vegetatively propagated, like the 'Prima Donna, Pink and Ruby Picotee" illustrated. Also popular are the seed-raised tuberous types that flower quickly, such as the popular Non-Stop range. These types are suitable for massed bedding. They flower all summer until cut back by frost. Height 23–30cm (9–12in). Tuber.

BRODIAEA LAXA

This North American plant is now more correctly called *Triteleia laxa*, but you may find it in catalogues under either name. The loose heads of funnel-shaped, pale blue flowers on wiry stems are long-lasting and make a good cut flower for early summer, but the plant lacks impact in a border. 'Koningin Fabiola' ('Queen Fabiola') is a purple-blue variety. Height 30–45cm (1–1¹/₂ ft). Corm.

■ ABOVE AND RIGHT
CANNA HYBRIDS

These exotic-looking plants from the warmer parts of North and South America have been described as the lazy gardener's delight. They come into bloom early and continue until the first frost, combining spectacular red, orange or yellow flowers with interesting foliage. Mostly the leaves are dark bronze or purple-bronze, but some are brightly variegated.

Being tender they have to be treated like dahlias, but they are not difficult to grow. Their tall height means they are usually most effective towards the back of a herbaceous border. Height 1.2–1.8m (4–6ft). Rhizome.

■ LEFT
CALADIUM BICOLOR

These are some of the few bulbs grown for foliage alone, their wonderfully marked, coloured leaves matching any show of flowers. Plants with pure white leaves veined green are sometimes named *C.* x *candidum*, or *C.* x *hortulanum*. There are many named varieties; the one illustrated is 'Red Flash'.

They are demanding tropical South American plants, and are usually grown in a conservatory or greenhouse where they can receive good light, and plenty of moisture and humidity.
Height 30–60cm (1–2ft). Tuber.

■ LEFT
COLCHICUM HYBRIDS

Some of the most striking colchicums are
the hybrids of garden origin. They come in
the usual colchicum colours – shades of
pink, and white. There are also doubles,
'Waterlily' being one of the best known.
The variety illustrated is 'The Giant'.
Height 15cm (6in), but leaves grow to
at least twice this height. Corm.

■ RIGHT AND ABOVE RIGHT
COLCHICUM SPECIOSUM

These remarkable plants from western and central Europe look like
huge crocuses. They bloom in early autumn, before the leaves
which appear in the spring, and have the curious characteristic of
being able to bloom even if they are not planted and are without
water. They live by drawing upon reserves in the bulb. There are
varieties in various shades of pink, as well as white. The variety
shown right is 'Album'. They are best grown beneath shrubs in
semi-shade, or in rough grass provided it is not too long and wild.
There are other colchicum species that flower at the same time,
such as *C. autumnale*, as well as the hybrids. Height 15cm (6in),
but leaves grow to at least twice this height. Corm.

■ ABOVE
CRINUM x POWELLII

This magnificent, late-flowering bulb is
probably a hybrid between two South
African species. The common name
sometimes used is Cape lily. The large
pink trumpet flowers span late summer
into autumn. Provide a warm, sunny
position, and in cold areas a protective
winter mulch. Although they are hardy
down to -18°C (0°F), avoid planting them
in cold areas. Height 1.2m (4ft). Bulb.

■ BELOW LEFT AND RIGHT, RIGHT
CROCOSMIA HYBRIDS

Crocosmias are outstanding border plants.
Many gardeners are only aware of the old
cottage garden favourite *C.* x *crocosmiiflora*
(montbretia), but there are a number of
modern hybrids, derived from South
African species. They are sometimes a little
less hardy and may need winter protection
in cold areas, but they have larger and
bolder flowers, and a large clump can be
one of the highlights of the late summer
border. There are many varieties, in shades
of orange, red and yellow. Height
75–90cm (2½–3ft). Corm.

■ LEFT
CROCUS SPECIOSUS

One of several autumn-flowering crocuses, this native of eastern Europe to the Caucasus and Iran comes in various shades of lilac and purple-blue. There is also a white. The flowers appear before the leaves, in early and mid-autumn. Try this pretty crocus under shrubs or in grass, in sun or semi-shade, where it can be left to multiply and naturalize. Height 10cm (4in). Corm.

■ RIGHT AND BELOW
CYCLAMEN HEDERIFOLIUM

One of the best known of the hardy miniature cyclamen, this Mediterranean species is tough and hardy and blooms prolifically in early autumn, continuing for months. The flowers come in various shades of pink, and there is also a white form. The ivy-shaped leaves are attractively patterned. It also has the virtue of thriving beneath trees, provided the ground receives some moisture in winter. You may find this species listed in catalogues under its older name of *C. neapolitanum*. It will self-seed, and naturalizes well. Height 7.5cm (3in). Corm.

CLASSIFYING DAHLIAS

There are specialist dahlia societies that classify the varieties according to the shape and size of their blooms, but these vary slightly from country to country. The dahlias illustrated here are only a small selection of the many kinds available. Within most groups there are small, medium and large varieties, determined by the diameter of the bloom. But even with so many different classifications there is a miscellaneous group for varieties that do not fit into other classifications.

If you simply want an attractive border plant that will flower for months and provide lots of flowers for cutting, just choose varieties that you find appealing. Do remember to check on their height because sizes vary from about 30cm (1ft) to over 1.5m (5ft). You only need worry about classifications if you plan to exhibit the bloom, in which case it is best to join a dahlia society.

The varieties available vary from year to year and from country to country, so shop around for the best.

■ ABOVE
DAHLIA, CACTUS

Cactus dahlias have double flowers and narrow petals that taper to a point, with the edges curved back for more than two-thirds of their length. This gives them a spiky appearance. The variety illustrated is 'Video'. Typical height: 90–120cm (3–4ft). Tuber.

■ LEFT
DAHLIA, SEMI-CACTUS

Semi-cactus dahlias have fully double flowers, with petals that curve backwards towards the tips, but they are flatter and broader than ordinary cactus varieties towards the base. They do look like cactus dahlias around the edge of the flower though, and more like a decorative variety in the centre. The variety illustrated is 'Hamari Katrina'. Typical height: 90–120cm (3–4ft). Tuber.

DAHLIA, LILLIPUT

These diminutive dahlias can be used as edgings or in tubs, troughs and large windowboxes. Most have single flowers, in all the usual dahlia colours, such as red, orange, pink, cream, and white. The variety illustrated is 'Omo'. Typical height: 30–45cm (1–1½ ft). Tuber.

■ ABOVE
DAHLIA, DECORATIVE

Decorative varieties have double flowers with flat petals that incurve a little at the edges, often reflexing back towards the stem. The group of decoratives described as waterlily varieties generally have fewer petals, which are flat and broad giving the flower a flatter appearance than normal decoratives. The variety illustrated is 'Kidd's Climax'. Typical height: 1.2–1.5m (4–5ft). Tuber.

■ LEFT
DAHLIA, COLLERETTE

The appearance is of a single flower with broad, open petals, usually between eight and ten, and a number of smaller petals arranged like a collar around the central disc. Shown here is 'Clair de Lune'. Typical height: 75–90cm (2½–3ft). Tuber.

FLOWERING TIME

The taller, large-flowering dahlias normally begin to flower in late summer and continue until the first frost. Small varieties bred for bedding or containers generally flower from midsummer and also continue until the first frost.

PLANTING AND OVERWINTERING

Dahlias are not frost hardy, but the tubers will be safe for a while even if an air frost kills the foliage. They must be lifted, however, before the frost has a chance to penetrate to tuber depth.

In areas where penetrating frosts do not occur, or are very rare, the tubers can be left in the ground. Elsewhere they must be lifted, dried off, and stored in a frost-proof space.

■ BELOW
DAHLIA, MISCELLANEOUS

Many excellent dahlias do not fall neatly into any of the more formal classifications, and are placed in this group by enthusiasts. The plants that have this label are not necessarily inferior, and there are many superb varieties that are great for summer beds and borders; the one illustrated is 'Bishop of Llandaff'. Seed-raised bedding varieties will form tubers by the end of the season, and can be lifted and replanted the following year, but they are usually raised afresh each season. Generally, named varieties propagated from cuttings or by division are superior for use in borders. Typical height: 45–60cm (1½–2ft). Tuber.

■ ABOVE
DAHLIA, POMPON AND BALL

Both pompon and ball dahlias have spherical blooms with tightly packed petals that are almost tubular at the base. Pompons are smaller with flowers no more than 5cm (2in) across. The variety shown is 'Candy Cupid', a miniature ball variety. Other common varieties include 'Kay Helen' (pompon) and 'Wootton Cupid' (miniature ball). Typical height: 90cm (3ft). Tuber.

DIERAMA PULCHERRIMUM

One of the most graceful of all the iris family, this South African plant deserves to be more widely planted. Two common names, angel's fishing rod and wand flower, give an indication of its elegant arching shoots, from which the pink to purple funnel-shaped flowers nod in a breeze. They do not transplant well and resent disturbance, so buy pot-grown plants if possible. Since the foliage is almost evergreen, they are seldom offered by bulb specialists as dry corms. Some specialist nurseries sell them as growing plants. Height 1–1.5m (3–5ft). Corm.

EREMURUS

Sometimes called foxtail lilies, these spectacular plants from western and central Asia are never ignored, for their tall flower spikes shooting up to 1.5m (5ft) or more look like the trail of a rocket. The colours are mainly pink, yellow or white, and there are various hybrids to try. The species illustrated is *E. himalaicus* from the north-west Himalayas. Early and midsummer is the usual flowering time. Plant the roots so that the central bud is about 5cm (2in) deep. Be patient, and avoid unnecessary disturbance once established. Height 1.2–2.1m (4–7ft). Rhizome.

■ ABOVE
GALTONIA CANDICANS

The so-called summer hyacinth is a South African plant, best seen in a herbaceous or mixed border where its bold spikes of white bells can make a statement in mid- or late summer. Leave undisturbed if possible to make a large clump. Where winters are cold, and the soil is likely to freeze deeply, it should be lifted for the winter and replanted in spring. Height 1–1.2m (3–4ft). Bulb.

■ ABOVE AND RIGHT
EUCOMIS BICOLOR

An invaluable plant to bring interest to a border in late summer and early autumn. In mild areas it will begin to flower in late summer, probably continuing into autumn, but in cold areas is best regarded as an autumn flower. This is one of several interesting species and hybrids that are available, most with green or greenish flowers, and all are worth growing. Even before the flowers appear, the tuft of leaves on top of the flower stem nestles in the centre of the plant like a pineapple, as shown on the right (hence its common name, pineapple lily). The tuft of leaves remains on top of the spike as it elongates (above), and flowering lasts for several weeks, followed by seedheads that are quite attractive. Height 30cm (1ft). Bulb.

■ BELOW
GLADIOLUS SPECIES

Several Gladiolus species are widely grown in gardens, but one of the most reliable is *G. byzantinus* (now more correctly called *G. communis* ssp. *byzantinus*), shown here. A Mediterranean species, it is best planted in the autumn for a display of reddish-purple flowers in early summer. The flowers are smaller and less perfectly formed than the hybrid gladioli usually grown, but they are tougher plants and hardy where the average winter minimum temperatures drop to -18°C (0°F). See *Acidanthera bicolor* for a description of *Gladiolus callianthus*. Height 45–75cm (1½–2½ft). Corm.

■ RIGHT
GLADIOLUS, BUTTERFLY

These are smaller than the large-flowered hybrids described right, with flowers 5–10cm (2–4in) across. There are many varieties, in a wide range of colours, usually with a contrasting blotch on the lower segments. The variety illustrated is 'Liebelei'. Butterfly gladioli are used for cutting and floral art. Treat in the same way as large-flowered varieties. Height 90cm (3ft). Corm.

■ ABOVE
GLADIOLUS, LARGE-FLOWERED

The large-flowered gladioli are derived from South African species and are the biggest and boldest, although spike height and flower size varies with variety. They are popular cut flowers, but can be rather stiff in a border unless planted in bold clumps with low-growing plants in front to hide the base of the stems. The colour range is very varied. Although there are a few long-established varieties, many new ones are introduced regularly and some are available only from a few specialist bulb companies. The variety illustrated is 'Green Woodpecker'. The flowering period ranges between midsummer and early autumn, depending on the variety and planting time. In areas where frosts penetrate to the depth of the corms, they should be lifted in autumn. Height 1–1.2m (3–4ft). Corm.

■ ABOVE
IRIS, DUTCH, ENGLISH AND SPANISH

All these bulbous iris are similar and are grown commercially as
cut flowers. They can also be used in summer borders, but need
to be planted in a clump, with low-growing plants in front, to
look really impressive. The flowering period is short, but by
growing all three kinds it is possible to spread the period of
interest. The iris illustrated is the Dutch variety 'Golden Harvest'.
Dutch irises, hybrids derived from species such as *I. xiphium* and
I. tingitana, flower in early summer, usually before the Spanish
type. Spanish irises, derived from *I. xiphium*, follow on from the
Dutch irises, flowering in early to midsummer. English irises,
derived from *I. latifolia* (*I. xiphioides*), flower in midsummer.
Height 60–90cm (2–3ft). Bulb.

■ ABOVE
HAEMANTHUS MULTIFLORUS

This native to tropical and South Africa is
more correctly called *Scadoxus multiflorus*.
Its common name is blood lily, alluding to
the red spots on the bulb. It can be left
outdoors in areas where only a few degrees
of frost are likely – elsewhere keep frost-
free in winter. An attractive pot plant, it
can be brought indoors when coming into
flower, being planted outdoors for the
summer. *Haemanthus multiflorus* ssp.
katherinae, usually listed simply as *H.
katherinae*, is a more robust plant that
grows to about 90cm (3ft). Height 60cm
(2ft). Bulb.

■ LEFT
IXIA

The African corn lily is usually sold as a
mixed hybrid, though the blue-green
I. viridiflora is sometimes available. *Ixia*
has long, thin stems that can look sparse in
a border, especially if there are no low-
growing plants in front to hide them. It is
therefore better as a cut flower than a
garden plant. The corms are usually lifted
in autumn and stored in a frost-free place
for replanting the following spring, and it
is only worth leaving them in the ground
in areas where frosts are light. The
flowering time is early or midsummer.
Height 45cm (1½ ft). Corm.

■ BELOW

LILIUM AURATUM

The golden-rayed lily is a Japanese species of great beauty, with large, fragrant white flowers, usually banded yellow and spotted red. The flowering period is late summer and early autumn, when a large clump can fill the air with fragrance. This species resents lime and should be grown in neutral or acid soils. Height 1–1.5m (3–5ft). Bulb.

■ ABOVE

LILIUM REGALE

Another classic lily, the regale is sure to make an impression on a border if grown in a large clump. The trumpet-like flowers in early and midsummer are mainly white, with a yellow inside throat, flushed purple-pink outside. There can be 20 or more fragrant flowers per stem. It is perhaps the best trumpet lily for the garden, and even a beginner should succeed. Height 1–1.5m (3–5ft). Bulb.

■ RIGHT

LILIUM, AMERICAN HYBRIDS

Hybrids of American species such as *L. pardalinum* are tough and reliable, and can usually fend for themselves for years. The famous 'Bellingham Hybrids' (illustrated) were introduced in 1933 in the USA. Today there are other hybrids, mainly with spotted yellow, yellow-red or orange nodding flowers. Height 1–1.5m (3–5ft). Bulb.

■ RIGHT
LILIUM, ORIENTAL HYBRIDS

This term covers hybrid lilies which derive mainly from Oriental species such as *L. auratum* and *L. speciosum*, usually flowering in late summer. The open shape of *L. auratum* is clearly in evidence in some of them, but others have more bowl-shaped flowers, or even flat or recurved shapes. This is due to the different species used in their hybridization. The variety illustrated is 'Le Reve'. Height 75–150cm (2½–5ft). Bulb.

■ LEFT
LILIUM, ASIATIC HYBRIDS

This loose term covers several different kinds of hybrid lilies. Some have upright flowers (like 'Chinook', illustrated), some outward-facing, others pendant. Although they vary in appearance, all come in the usual range of lily colours, such as yellows, pinks, reds and whites, and make reliable garden plants for borders. The compact varieties also do well in patio pots. Mid- and late summer is the normal flowering period. Height 60–90cm (2–3ft). Bulb.

LILY GROUPS

The *International Lily Register* divides lilies into nine main groups, though some of these have three or four sub-divisions. You will sometimes see these groups referred to in catalogues (VIIa, for example, means hybrids of Far Eastern species such as *L. auratum* or *L. speciosum* with trumpet-shaped flowers), but catalogues and lily enthusiasts are more likely to use names such as Asiatic Hybrids or Orientals than numbers.

■ ABOVE
LILIUM, TRUMPET HYBRIDS

Many hybrids have a bloom with a distinctive trumpet shape, and make pleasing border plants. They derive mainly from Asiatic species. Usually pleasantly fragrant, yellow, white and pink are the most common colours. Mid- and late summer is the usual flowering period. Height 1.2–1.5m (4–5ft). Bulb.

■ LEFT

NERINE BOWDENII

This South African bulb is one of the very
best autumn flowers, beginning to bloom
in mid-autumn and sometimes continuing
into early winter. Since the spidery-looking
pink flowers appear before the leaves, the
display can appear to burst upon the
autumn scene quite suddenly. Hardier
than most other nerines, it should be
suitable for areas where the average
minimum temperature does not fall below
-7°C (20°F), especially if given a little
protection. Height 45–60cm (1¹/₂–2ft).

■ ABOVE

OXALIS

The species illustrated is *O. triangularis* ssp. *papilionacea*. Plant
outdoors only where the average minimum temperature does not
fall below -7°C (20°F). Height 10cm (4in). Rhizome (*O.
triangularis*), tuber (*O. tetraphylla*).

■ LEFT

ORNITHOGALUM THYRSOIDES

The chincherinchee excels as a cut flower. The flower spikes will
last for up to three weeks if cut in bud. Grow in a frost-free
greenhouse or conservatory. Height 30–45cm (1–1¹/₂ ft). Bulb.

■ LEFT

RHODOHYPOXIS BAURII

This charming South African plant is a dwarf for the rock garden, or for growing in a shallow trough or bonsai pot. The flowers, in shades from white to rose-pink, held just above the hairy grass-like foliage, appear for a long period over most of the summer. The variety illustrated is the hybrid 'Dawn'. It is hardy to about -5°C (23°F). If colder, lift the tubers for the winter and store in peat or vermiculite. Height 7.5cm (3in). Tuber.

■ ABOVE AND LEFT

RANUNCULUS ASIATICUS

These colourful plants related to the buttercup originate in the eastern Mediterranean, but have been highly bred to produce double blooms in a wide range of colours. In the garden they flower in summer, but they can be flowered earlier as pot plants using dwarf varieties. Seed-raised varieties are available that flower within a year. Lift and store the tubers dry in winter in cold areas. Height 45–60cm (1½–2ft). Tuber.

■ RIGHT
SCHIZOSTYLIS COCCINEA

Though commonly called the kaffir lily it is a pretty member of the iris family, and has the merit of flowering in early and mid-autumn, precisely when bright flowers are beginning to be scarce. The species is scarlet, but there are varieties in various shades of red or pink. Height 45–60cm (1½–2ft). Rhizome.

■ BELOW
SCILLA PERUVIANA

This Mediterranean plant blooms in early summer, and has an impact beyond its compact size. Grow it at the front of a herbaceous border or in front of shrubs. It is hardy to about -5°C (23°F), but is only likely to thrive where winters are relatively mild and penetrating frosts unlikely. Height 15–25cm (6–10in). Bulb.

■ ABOVE
STERNBERGIA LUTEA

From a distance this plant looks like a yellow crocus, though this native of the Mediterranean is actually related to the amaryllis. It flowers in early and mid-autumn and is best grown where it can be left undisturbed for several years in a place where it will not be swamped by larger-growing plants. Height 10–15cm (4–6in). Bulb.

■ LEFT
TIGRIDIA PAVONIA

The tiger flower from Mexico has fleeting flowers that last less than a day in perfect conditions, but fortunately there is usually a succession of them. Despite this shortcoming, the blooms are so distinctive and exotic-looking that they demand attention. Colours include yellow, orange, scarlet, pink, cream and lilac. Usually they are heavily spotted or marked. They start flowering in early summer and will continue to produce a few flowers in mid- or late summer. Despite their exotic appearance, they can be left in the soil if the winters are not severe. Height 30–60cm (1–2ft). Bulb.

■ RIGHT
ZANTEDESCHIA AETHIOPICA

The calla lily, which is not a true lily but an aroid, is a South African plant that is hardy only to about -7ºC (20ºF), which limits its use in the garden in cold areas, though it makes a fine conservatory or greenhouse plant with its distinctive white flowers. It is a good pondside plant, though it will also grow in an ordinary border. It can be grown as a bog plant or even covered with up to 30cm (1ft) of water. 'Crowborough' is considered to be hardier than other forms of the plant, but 'Green Goddess' has very unusual and attractive green and white spathes. Height 60–90cm (2–3ft). Rhizome.

The Grower's Guide

Buying bulbs

Buying bulbs is part of the excitement of gardening, part of that vital anticipation that extends the pleasure.

You can usually rely on spring bulbs to flower in the first season, and while this is true of the majority of summer types, such as dahlias, gladioli and tigridias, some of the less common types may not bloom in the first season, or the performance may be below expectations. For that reason, if using a type that you have not grown before, do not plant it in a prime position that will look bare if it does not bloom.

Fortunately, most summer bulbs are planted in herbaceous or mixed borders and some can be left to form large clumps over the years. They are best regarded as a long-term investment that will perform for many years.

Although the majority of autumn-flowering bulbs are hardy, many summer-flowering types native to

■ ABOVE
Mail order bulbs may arrive in paper or plastic bags or be packed in sawdust, wood shavings or peat. Unpack as soon as possible and plant once any danger of a frost has passed.

Achimenes tubers (scaly rhizomes) are easily crushed and may be packed in peat. As they are a similar colour the rhizomes can be difficult to see; empty the packet into a small container and search through the material.

It is sometimes possible to buy tuberous begonias from garden centres as growing plants, which is useful if you want them for summer bedding and do not have a greenhouse in which to start them off as tubers.

countries like South Africa are not. Always check whether you need to lift them in the autumn, keeping them out of the frost.

All the common bulbs are available from good garden centres, but if you want to grow a particular variety of gladiolus, for example, you may have to send for specialist bulb catalogues. Bulb specialists usually offer a wide range of dahlias too, but enthusiasts often buy young plants raised from cuttings from specialist dahlia nurseries. This is usually only necessary if you want to grow for exhibition or have set your heart on a particular variety that you have seen, as there is no shortage of excellent varieties sold as tubers.

There is one big advantage in buying from garden centres or shops: you can check the condition of loose bulbs, and avoid any about which you have doubts. On the other hand there is a greater chance of varieties becoming muddled where other shoppers have picked them up and replaced them in the wrong container. This is less of a problem with pre-packed bulbs.

Mail order companies are likely to offer a wider range of varieties and usually offer newer ones, too. Some companies may send out larger bulbs,

which are more likely to flower well in the first season, though this is not universally the case.

Autumn-flowering bulbs

If ordering autumn-flowering bulbs from an autumn catalogue, send your order in early. Those that bloom in early autumn, such as colchicums and *Crocus speciosus*, should be ordered in time to be planted by late summer.

Some autumn-flowering bulbs, such as nerines and schizostylis, are usually sold and planted in spring. Do not be alarmed if these do not appear to grow as quickly as other bulbs, as they may remain dormant for a few months before the first signs of growth become visible.

■ ABOVE
Occasionally nerines are sold in the green, with their leaves intact. This is a good way to buy them provided they have not been allowed to dry out.

■ ABOVE
Do not judge a bulb by size alone. Gladioli vary greatly in size according to type. *Gladiolus nanus* corms (bottom) are always smaller than those of the large-flowered hybrids (top).

Planting bulbs

Summer bulbs vary enormously in their requirements. Whenever possible follow the planting advice on the packet or in the catalogue. The advice given here is appropriate for the majority of bulbs, but individual plants may have their own specific needs.

Bulbs and corms

Since corms and true bulbs can generally be covered with twice their own depth of soil, a hole 7.5cm (3in) deep is appropriate for a bulb 2.5cm (1in) from base to tip. Often the planting depth is not critical, so there is no need to measure each planting hole once you have an idea of the approximate planting depth.

A few bulbs, mainly late-flowering kinds from warm climates, such as crinums and nerines, are normally planted with the nose of the bulb just below the surface. This helps by exposing the bulbs to more warmth from the sun, but it may mean winter protection in the form of a mulch is required in cold areas. Remove the mulch in spring.

Tubers

These vary tremendously in size and shape, and it is difficult to generalize about planting depth. Those with a cluster of tubers that meet in a crown at the top are generally best planted shallowly, with the top of the tuber just below soil level.

With some major exceptions, such as tuberous begonias and gloxinias (sinningia), which are usually planted with the top of the tuber sitting flush with the surface of the ground and the top exposed, individual tubers are

■ RIGHT
Nerines are among the best of all autumn-flowering plants, but for best results they should be planted shallowly in a warm position. Shown here is 'Fenwick's Variety'.

usually planted so that they are covered with soil equal to once to twice their own depth.

Plant elongated tubers horizontally, and claw-shaped ones such as ranunculus with the "claws" pointing downwards.

Rhizomes

Unless the instructions on the packet or in the catalogue advise otherwise, plant rhizomes horizontally, and cover with soil equal to about their own depth. Rhizomatous irises, especially the popular bearded irises of borders, are planted with the top of the rhizome exposed.

Preparing the ground

Deep-rooted perennial weeds are difficult to eradicate from around bulbs without disturbing the clumps, so make sure the ground is as weed-free as possible before planting.

Bulbs that flower in summer will be growing during the warm months, and they require a generous application of a general balanced fertilizer. This is preferable to something slow-acting, such as bone meal, which is often used when planting spring-flowering bulbs.

DIGGING AND WEEDING

1 Fork over the soil, removing as many weeds as possible before planting. If difficult or deep-rooted weeds are present, remove the roots as you fork over the soil. The hoe is a hazardous tool to use among emerging bulbs.

2 Dig over the soil with a fork or spade. Most bulbs, especially dahlias, will benefit if plenty of organic material, such as garden compost or well-rotted manure, is dug in at the same time. On heavy soil fork in coarse grit to improve the drainage.

3 All bulbs planted in spring will benefit from feeding. Fork, hoe or rake in a balanced general fertilizer.

4 After digging over the soil, rake the ground level before planting, breaking down large clods of soil at the same time.

Planting in borders

Borders are the ideal place for the majority of summer-flowering bulbs, especially those with a short flowering season, such as galtonias and gladioli, as the uninteresting foliage can be hidden by bushier border plants.

If planting among other plants in an established border, it is best to wait until the herbaceous plants are just coming through in order to determine the most suitable planting positions for the bulbs. For minimal disturbance to surrounding plants, prepare an area of ground just large enough to accommodate the clump.

PLANTING BULBS IN BORDERS

1 When planting in an existing border, excavate sufficient soil to plant a clump of bulbs, then add a soil improver such as peat or peat substitute, or garden compost.

2 With poorly drained soil, or bulbs particularly prone to rotting, it is worth adding a layer of coarse sand or grit in the base of the planting hole.

3 Fork in a balanced general fertilizer, mixing it thoroughly with the soil, at the rate recommended by the manufacturer. A slow-release fertilizer can be used if you prefer.

4 Plant at the spacing and depth recommended on the packet or in the catalogue (these are lilies). If no recommendation is given, cover with twice the bulb's own depth.

5 If you are likely to hoe or cultivate the area before the shoots emerge, insert a small cane beside each bulb as a marker, then finish returning the soil. Remember to insert a label.

■ BELOW
Lilies look particularly pleasing among herbaceous plants, which
help to hide their rather uninteresting stems. They pack plenty of
impact into a very small space.

Bulbs in patio tubs

There are so many colourful summer flowers for containers that only the most magnificent bulbs should be chosen for patio pots, unless you are a bulb enthusiast and do not mind a summer of watering and care for what may be a fleeting display.

Lilies are the number one candidate for planting in patio pots. There are small varieties for small containers, and tall ones for big pots. The display may last only a week or two, but while in bloom they will be among the most stunning plants in the garden.

WHAT TO TRY IN PATIO POTS

Although most bulbs can be grown in pots, it is best to restrict the choice to those that will provide the brightest, longest, or most interesting display. Also note that a few, such as nerines, are best left in the pot for a few years before they flower well.

- *Agapanthus*
- Tuberous begonias
- Dahlias (dwarf varieties)
- *Eucomis*
- *Haemanthus*
- Lilies

■ ABOVE

Although the modern hybrids, and especially the dwarf varieties, are likely to be brighter and bolder, some of the taller species, like these *Lilium regale*, create a cool elegance that has its own special charm.

PLANTING LILIES IN A PATIO POT

1 The more lilies that you can pack into the pot, the bolder and more spectacular the display, so choose a pot at least 25cm (10in) across, preferably more. Make sure it has a drainage hole, which should be covered to prevent the potting soil washing through.

2 Cover the drainage hole with a piece of broken pot or a stone, then cover with a shallow layer of gravel to ensure good drainage. If you don't have any gravel handy, use coarse chopped bark instead.

3 Place sufficient potting soil in the base to raise the level to a height that will allow the bulbs to be covered with twice their own depth, and still leave a 12–25mm ($\frac{1}{2}$–1in) gap between soil and rim for watering.

4 Plant about three or five bulbs, depending on the size of the pot and bulb, then cover them with more potting soil, firming it gently between the bulbs. Leave sufficient space between the top of the soil and the rim of the pot for easy watering (see step 3).

5 A slow-release fertilizer will ensure strong growth. Granules are best mixed with the potting soil, but pellets like these can be placed beneath the bulbs or pushed into the soil after planting them. Cover the surface with a mulch of gravel and label. Water thoroughly and allow to drain.

Transform patios with a well-placed pot plant, such as this attractive *Lilium regale*.

Growing for cut flowers

Many bulbs make excellent cut flowers. Florists almost always have a stock of various cut flowers grown from bulbs, which shows their value for floral displays. Bulbous irises (Dutch, English and Spanish varieties), lilies, and gladioli are among the most widely grown in gardens, but there are many others to try (see Box at right).

■ BELOW
This wonderful bunch of cut flowers includes some magnificent lilies, but the blue flowers are brodiaeas (sometimes called triteleias), which are also grown from bulbs.

Planting for cutting

If you require only a small number of stems for cutting, it is best to take them from clumps in the borders and around the garden, but when a large number of stems are required it is worth using a spare corner of the garden to plant in rows for cutting. Often the bulbs can be planted more closely than normal to save space. If you have a greenhouse, try growing a few of the plants suggested in the greenhouse border, for earlier blooms.

WHAT TO GROW FOR CUTTING

- *Alstroemeria* hybrids
- *Brodiaea*
- *Crocosmia*
- *Dahlia*
- *Eremurus*
- *Gladiolus*
- *Iris* – Dutch, English, Spanish
- *Lilium*
- *Nerine*
- *Ornithogalum thyrsoides* (chincherinchee)
- *Polianthes tuberosa*
- *Schizostylis*
- *Zantedeschia aethiopica*

■ BELOW

Summer brings an abundance of varied and beautiful material for the flower arranger. This mixed arrangement uses lilies to dramatic effect.

BLOCKS AND CLUMPS

Some cut flowers are more conveniently grown in blocks rather than rows. Use this system for plants that grow into one another rather than upright ones like gladioli or irises. Alstroemerias and zantedeschias are conveniently planted in blocks. However, clump-forming plants such as crocosmias and schizostylis are best grown in clumps, in a spare piece of ground or the flower border.

PLANTING IN ROWS FOR CUTTING

1 If planning to grow the bulbs in the same place for several years, hoe in a general balanced fertilizer, then place the bulbs (here gladiolus corms) in the bottom of the trench. For convenience, plant those with upright growth in double rows.

2 Cover the bulbs by shovelling back the excavated soil, or draw it back with a hoe, being careful not to disturb them.

3 Mark the position of the row with canes, to enable surface weeding to take place before the bulbs come through. Remember to insert a label.

Naturalizing bulbs

Although few summer-flowering bulbs are naturalized in grass, there are some delightful autumn-flowering species that can be used. True crocuses such as *C. speciosus* and *C. nudiflorus* can be planted in short grass, while colchicums (sometimes called autumn crocuses, though they are much larger and not true crocuses) can look spectacular.

Plant them where the grass can be left unmown while the leaves are present (which means spring for some of the crocuses and colchicums), and in a position that can be left untrimmed from late summer or early autumn once the flower buds begin to emerge.

The steps here show colchicums being planted, but crocuses can be treated in the same way, though they will require shallower planting.

Colchicums, such as *C.* 'Waterlily', can look spectacular naturalized in grass.

NATURALIZING COLCHICUMS

1 Scatter the corms so that they look informal and natural (avoid planting in a regular pattern such as a block). A bulb planter is useful for removing a core of grass and soil from a lawn.

2 Make sure the planting hole is wide enough to take the corm without it becoming wedged, and deep enough to be covered with at least its own depth of soil.

3 Ensure the corm is in contact with the soil at the base, then release the core of soil from the planter. It may be necessary to remove a little soil from the base of the plug so that it fits back into the hole.

4 Press the plug of soil firmly back into the hole, leaving the top flush with the surrounding surface if possible.

Propagation

It is usually much easier – and certainly a lot quicker – to buy flowering-sized bulbs than to attempt to propagate your own, but propagation can be fun and raising your own plants gives one a great sense of achievement. Dividing a clump of established bulbs gives you more flowering-sized plants instantly, and propagation does not come easier than that.

Raising seedlings will provide a large number of plants cheaply, but it is usually slow. There are other techniques for raising certain kinds of bulbs, such as growing lilies from scales, that will give you more plants than division. This is also quicker than raising seedlings (and there is no worry about whether they will be like their parents).

Dividing tubers

Tubers can be divided provided each piece has an "eye" (growth bud). Dahlia tubers that form a crown will not grow if individual tubers are separated without an attached growth bud – if the group is divided with a sharp knife it is important to ensure that each has a piece of main stem and a growth bud attached.

Begonia and gloxinia tubers, shown below, are easy to divide. Both tubers can be treated in the same way.

Dividing clumps

Clumps of established bulbs, corms or tubers provide a simple means of propagation.

The best time to divide established clumps is after the leaves have died back, or after flowering if they have persistent leaves.

Lift the clump with a fork, being careful not to spear or damage it, and shake off most of the soil. Pull the clump apart and replant, arranging the sections fairly close together if you have a lot and want quick impact, or spacing them out more to allow for future growth. Replant at their original depth.

DIVIDING A BEGONIA

1 Cut the tuber with a sharp knife, making sure each piece has a bud. These are easier to detect when the tubers are about to start into growth.

2 Dip the cut surface into a fungicide to reduce the risk of the tuber rotting. A sulphur dust is suitable, though other fungicides can be used.

3 Pot up the pieces of tuber as you would normally, but keep an eye on them to ensure a fungal infection does not become established.

■ RIGHT
Small bulb offsets are often produced around the base of a mature bulb (here a muscari). Simply detach and grow on.

Dividing rhizomes

Plants with rhizomes are best divided when the leaves die down, or after flowering if the foliage is persistent.

Lift the clump with a fork and shake off any surplus soil. Tease out the rhizomes, and cut into smaller sections, then replant at their original depth. Rhizomes usually grow horizontally, but if you accidentally plant vertically they will probably still grow.

Cuttings

Dahlias and begonias are among the few plants that can be raised from cuttings, and this will give more plants than propagation by dividing the tuber.

Start tuberous begonias into growth in trays, then remove the shoot with a bit of the tuber attached. Pot up.

Lay the tubers in deep trays of potting soil in a greenhouse in late winter. When the new shoots are a couple of inches long, take cuttings to root in the usual way.

Offsets

A large number of true bulbs produce offsets (small bulbs around the base of the old one). These will eventually separate from the parent bulbs, but you can remove them while small and grow them in a spare piece of ground until they reach flowering size. They are best removed and replanted when the leaves die down.

Corms, such as gladioli, sometimes produce a large number of cormlets around the base of the old corm. If detached and grown for a couple of years, they will reach flowering size and can then be planted in the border.

Bulbs from seed

This is a useful method if you require a large number of bulbs at little cost, perhaps for naturalizing. Since hybrids and named varieties are unlikely to produce plants the same as their parents, it is best to restrict seed-sowing to species.

If you save your own seed, sow as soon as possible but be prepared to wait for germination. Some bulbs may be slow to germinate. If possible, keep the pots or trays in a cold frame, but do not forget to water them.

When large enough, grow the seedlings in a spare piece of ground for a couple of years, then move to their flowering positions.

Seeds can be sown in trays or pots, but be prepared to be patient. Keep them in a cold frame to germinate.

PROPAGATING LILIES FROM SCALES

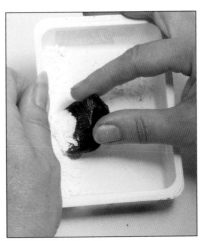

1 Lilies can be propagated by treating the scales like cuttings. Remove healthy scales (the individual segments that form a bulb), being careful not to damage them.

2 Dip the exposed surface into a fungicide to reduce the risk of the tissue rotting before the scale can root.

3 Insert the scales in a seed tray containing vermiculite or a sandy rooting mixture (it must be free-draining), leaving the tips exposed.

4 If the tray is kept in a warm place shoots will begin to appear after a few weeks to a couple of months. Do not allow the rooting mixture to dry out, but avoid over-watering, and keep in good light once shoots appear.

5 When the scales have rooted well and two or more leaves have developed, plant them in the garden, in a spare piece of ground where they can be grown for a couple of seasons.

STEM BULBLETS

Some lilies produce small bulbs where the leaves join the stem. Once these have reached the size where they begin to drop off, you can collect them and pot them up or plant them out in a piece of spare ground. They will produce new plants that should flower after a couple of years.

Examples of lilies that produce stem bulblets, sometimes called bulbils, are *L. tigrinum* and *L. bulbiferum*, as well as hybrids derived from them.

Bulbcare

Bulbs, including corms and tubers, have a natural reserve of nutrients that they can draw upon. This is the reason why colchicums, for example, will flower without even being planted, and why hyacinths can flower in water – but they will always respond to extra care and attention.

Feeding

Even bulbs that give an impressive performance the first season after planting may deteriorate rapidly in future years unless the plants are fed during the growing season. The majority of summer and autumn bulbs can be fed with a general balanced fertilizer that you should use on all flower beds and borders in spring or early summer.

Only a few, such as dahlias, require supplementary feeding through the growing seasons, and even this is not essential for a general garden display. It is best to feed all bulbs at least once a year, using a balanced general fertilizer.

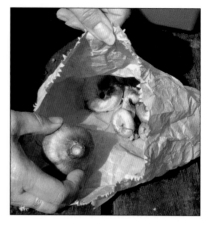

■ ABOVE
Store gladiolus corms in paper bags, or in trays, in a frost-free place. Do not forget to label them.

LIFTING AND STORING GLADIOLI

1 At the end of the season, loosen the soil and lift gladiolus corms carefully. To save and grow the cormlets around the base, take care not to pull the corms out of the ground roughly. Cut off most of the stem, leaving a stub attached to the corm.

2 Place the lifted corms in a shed or greenhouse to dry. Once the old stem has dried, usually after a week or two, break it or cut it off with secateurs (pruners), being careful not to damage the corm.

3 Remove the small cormlets from around the base of the corm. If you want to grow them, store them separately and plant out in spring; otherwise discard them. Break off the old shrivelled corm at the base of the new one, and discard.

Dead-heading

Most bulbs require dead-heading, if only to improve their appearance. In the case of those that flower for a long period, such as dahlias and cannas, it will help to ensure continuity of flower and probably larger blooms too.

Remove spent thick stems, for example on gladioli, or large individual blooms, as on dahlias, with secateurs (pruners), but many can be trimmed back simply with shears – crocosmias, for example.

Lifting and storing

Some summer-flowering bulbs that we grow in the garden are frost-tender, such as tuberous begonias. Others that are well protected beneath the ground may survive where the ground is not frozen deeply, but they will be lost in a very cold winter. Gladioli and dahlias fall into this category.

Except where winters are very mild, and frosts do not penetrate more than a few centimetres (an inch or so) into the soil, it is best to lift gladioli, and other vulnerable bulbs, and store them in a cool, frost-proof place over winter.

LIFTING AND STORING DAHLIA TUBERS

1 Lift dahlia tubers once frost has blackened the foliage. To make the job easier, first cut off the stems about 15cm (6in) above the ground, and remove stakes.

2 Use a fork to lift the clump of tubers, inserting it far enough away to avoid the risk of spearing the tubers. If possible, do it when the soil is fairly dry.

3 Carefully remove as much soil as possible before taking the tubers into a shed or greenhouse to dry off. This will be easier if the soil is not too wet.

4 The tubers are likely to store better if they are suspended to dry for about a week. Once the old stem has dried, cut it off just above the tubers.

Pests and other problems

Fortunately bulbs are prone to few serious pests, and most are confined to certain types of plants, such as lilies or dahlias. Vigilance and prompt action, however, should keep all your bulbs in good health if you know what to look for.

Aphids

How to identify: Of the many kinds of aphids, those most likely to be troublesome are the common greenfly and blackfly, which will be visible on the plants. They will attack a wide range of bulbs, particularly dahlias and lilies, weakening the plants and spreading virus diseases.
Cause: Endemic populations.
Control and prevention: Spray with an appropriate insecticide.

Lily beetle

How to identify: The adult lily beetle is bright red and about 6mm ($^1/_4$in) long. The grubs (larvae) are like orange-red maggots with black heads, but they cover themselves with their own black excrement. Both the grubs and adult beetles can devastate a plant by eating the leaves and even flowers.
Cause: This is a major pest for lilies in some areas. The adult beetles over-winter in plant debris.
Control and prevention: Remove the beetles by hand first, then spray the plants with an insecticide to control the larvae.

■ ABOVE
The lily beetle is quite attractive, but do not be deceived. It can inflict terrible damage.

■ RIGHT
These lily blooms have been attacked by lily beetle larvae, which have already stripped the foliage.

Slugs and snails

How to identify: Slugs that live underground can damage tubers and bulbs, those that live above ground may cause limited damage to the shoots as they emerge. Snails may be a problem for dahlias even when fully grown.
Cause: There are many species of slugs and snails, most of them harmful to plants. Not all species of slug live above ground, a few live in the soil.
Control and prevention: Use baits or traps. If they are a major problem, try a biological control.

■ LEFT
Dahlias are often dusted with an insecticide such as derris (rotenone) to control earwigs, and a range of other pests. Spray the leaves with water first so that the dust adheres well.

Viruses

How to identify: These are impossible to see, so you can judge an infection only by the symptoms. These include stunted growth and distorted leaves; on some plants the foliage may be mottled or unevenly coloured. Growth is generally poor.
Cause: Viruses are microscopic pathogenic agents capable of rapid reproduction within the cells of the host plant. They are usually transmitted by sap-sucking insects.
Control and prevention: Dig up and burn affected plants. Make sure insects, such as aphids, are controlled, as these spread virus diseases.

■ ABOVE
Bulbs are particularly vulnerable to slug damage when the succulent shoots emerge from the ground.

Botrytis

How to identify: Commonly known as grey mould, this widespread fungal disease causes a fluffy grey mould to grow on dying flowers or affected foliage. It can spread to the bulbs.
Cause: Particular species of botrytis cause specific diseases in some bulbs (such as tulip fire in tulips), but the widespread species described here is *Botrytis cinerea*. Poor garden hygiene, overcrowding or lack of air circulation may invite an attack.
Control and prevention: Lift and burn the plant if the actual bulb is affected; if only the leaves, buds or flower are affected, apply a systemic fungicide.

Bulb and corm rots

How to identify: Several diseases can cause rotting in bulbs, corms and tubers, but it will be difficult to determine the specific organism. Rotting is likely if bulbs are soft at the base when you buy them, or if patches of bare earth are left where the bulbs have not come through.
Cause: Various fungi and bacteria are responsible, causing similar symptoms.
Control and prevention: Do not plant any bulbs that feel soft if you press them gently. Soaking bulbs in a fungicide solution before planting may help. Burn any bulbs that do not emerge from the ground, and do not replant with new bulbs in the same area.

■ ABOVE
Slugs and snails usually come out to feed at night, like those here feasting on dahlias. Find them with a torch, and destroy them.

Calendar

Late winter to early spring

- If you are planning to order by mail, send off for catalogues.
- If you are not looking for uncommon bulbs, look in seed catalogues. Many seed companies offer a range of popular bulbs.
- For dahlia cuttings start tubers into growth in trays in the greenhouse.
- Start pot plants, such as gloxinias and achimenes, into growth.
- For begonia cuttings, start into growth in trays in the greenhouse.

Mid-spring

- Plant tender bulbs, such as gladioli, in areas where late frosts are unlikely.
- Place gladioli corms in seed trays, kept in a light, warm position, to encourage early shooting. Plant out in late spring or early summer.

Late spring

- Plant summer-flowering bulbs.
- Divide established clumps of autumn-flowering bulbs.
- Plant dahlia tubers if frosts are unlikely by the time the shoots emerge. If frosts do occur, protect the shoots.
- Plant any lilies which were not planted in the autumn.

Early summer

- Finish planting summer bulbs as soon as possible, but do not expose the growth of tender ones to the frost.
- Plant out tuberous begonias that were started into growth in the greenhouse, once frost is unlikely.
- Apply a balanced fertilizer to bulbs that are now growing vigorously.
- Plant out dahlia plants raised from cuttings, once frost is unlikely.
- Stake tall plants, such as tall varieties of gladioli, growing in exposed positions if necessary.

■ **LEFT**
Bulbs, corms and tubers being over-wintered in a frost-free place should be checked once a month. Early detection will help prevent any rot spreading to others.

■ **RIGHT**
If you want large dahlia flowers, remove the side buds on each stem.

Midsummer

- Feed with a balanced general fertilizer if not already done.
- Water in dry spells if growth seems slow or retarded. Then mulch to conserve moisture.
- Feed and water bulbs in pots and containers regularly. Water may be required daily, and it is worth using a liquid feed every week unless a slow-release fertilizer was originally used at planting time.
- Dead-head regularly.
- Propagate lilies from scales (it can be done at other times, but mid-summer propagation is usually very successful).

Late summer

● Continue to dead-head.
● Send for spring-flowering bulb catalogues. They usually contain some autumn-flowering bulbs too.
● Order and plant autumn-flowering bulbs now.
● Save seed of those plants you wish to propagate this way. Collect it when ripe but before it is shed. If you gather the seeds when they are ripe, it is often possible to shake them directly into an envelope. Clean and label before sowing or storing.
● Propagate lilies from scales – it can be done at other times, but late summer is usually very successful.

● Start to disbud dahlias if you want large blooms. This is not necessary for bedding dahlias.

Early autumn

● Plant autumn-flowering bulbs without delay.
● Plant lilies to flower next summer.
● Continue to save seed of those plants you wish to propagate this way. Clean and label.
● Propagate lilies from bulblets and stem bulbils, planting them in a spare piece of ground.
● In cold areas, lift frost-tender bulbs that lie near the surface, such as tuberous begonias, before the first frost is forecast. Those protected by a layer of soil can be left until frost has blackened or killed the foliage.

Mid-autumn

● Lift tender bulbs and store in a dry, frost-free place, after drying them and removing the soil. Dahlias can usually be left to flower until the foliage is blackened by frost. Suspend the lifted

■ LEFT AND RIGHT
Harvest seeds by cutting the heads when the seeds begin to ripen, but before they fall. Place in a paper bag until ready for cleaning. Remember to label.

tubers upside down for the stems to dry off before storing.
● Mulch those of borderline hardiness that may survive outdoors with a little extra frost protection.
● Divide established clumps if they have become large, or if you need to divide them for propagation purposes.

Winter

● Check stored bulbs, corms or tubers periodically, and remove any showing signs of softness or rot. This will help to prevent the disease or rot spreading to others in close proximity.
● Walk around the garden and plan your planting scheme for next year.
● Order bulb catalogues as soon as they become available, and place your order early if possible.

Other recommended plants

Allium giganteum

Amaryllis belladonna

Anemones

Chlidanthus fragrans

Achimenes Sometimes called the hot water plant because they do not like being given cold water. Hybrids with a cascading habit are suitable for hanging baskets. The flowers, in shades of purple, blue and pink, appear all summer. Height 30cm (1ft), or trailing. Scaly rhizome.

Agapanthus hybrids These magnificent plants have fleshy roots and are usually available from nurseries selling herbaceous plants. The ball-shaped flower heads in shades of blue, sometimes white, make splendid features in mid- and late summer. Height 90–120cm (3–4ft).

Allium giganteum Perhaps the largest and most striking allium, with 15cm (6in) heads of pinkish-purple on tall stems in early summer, ideal for growing towards the back of a border, preferably in full sun. From central Asia. Height 1.5–1.8m (5–6ft).

Allium schubertii This native of the eastern Mediterranean and central Asia has large heads of star-shaped pink or purple flowers in early summer. It is best in full sun, towards the front of a border. Height 30–60cm (1–2ft).

Alstroemeria hybrids These so-called Peruvian lilies are not true lilies; they grow from elongated thickened roots and not bulbs. The showy flowers are often multi-coloured and are excellent for cutting. Where winters are severe they should be lifted and replanted the following spring. Height 60–90cm (2–3ft).

Amaryllis belladonna Not to be confused with the similar hippeastrum used mainly as an indoor pot plant, which has the common name of amaryllis. This one bears large pink trumpet flowers from late summer into autumn. A native of South Africa, it flowers on leafless stems, the

glossy strap-like leaves appearing when the flowers have finished. Height 75–90cm (2½–3ft). Bulb.

Anemone coronaria This is the popular florist's anemone, the single De Caen and double St Brigid groups being the ones usually seen. Plant in early or mid-spring in a sunny position and in well-drained soil for early and mid-summer flowering. Height 23cm (9in).

Arisaema tortuosum This native of the Himalayas is sometimes called the cobra lily because the flowers arch over at the top and resemble a cobra's head. They are tuberous plants that grow very well in shady areas. The green spathes of this majestic species appear in midsummer. Height 90cm (3ft).

Begonia, tuberous hybrids The large-flowered tuberous-rooted begonias are sold as tubers, but some types, such

as the Non-Stop series, can be raised from seed. There are both upright and trailing kinds in shades of yellow, red, pink and white. They bloom from summer into autumn, if watered and fed regularly. Height 30–60cm (1–2ft).

Cardiocrinum giganteum Sometimes called the giant lily because of its tall stature. Each flower stalk carries up to 20 fragrant trumpet flowers 15cm (6in) across, in mid- and late summer. Not an easy bulb to grow, it requires partial shade and deeply dug soil that does not dry out too readily in summer, as well as partial shade. The bulb dies after it has flowered, and the new offset bulbs usually take about three years to flower. Height 1.8–2.4m (6–8ft).

Chlidanthus fragrans This uncommon bulb comes from the Andes mountains, and its yellow summer flowers resemble a small daffodil.

Dachtylorhiza elata

Hemerocallis 'Wind Song'

Homeria ochroleuca

Hymenocallis x *festalis*

They have a lily-like fragrance. The bulbs are best lifted before the first frost arrives. They can also be grown in pots. In either case, leave the neck of the bulb exposed when planting. Height 25cm (10in).

Dactylorhiza elata This is just one representative of several pleasing, tuberous orchids available from specialist nurseries or bulb suppliers. This is a Mediterranean species that flowers in late spring and early summer, the flower colour varying from pink to maroon. Grow undisturbed in damp ground in partial shade. Height 30–45cm (1–1½ ft).

Dracunculus vulgaris A member of the arum family, this strange tuberous plant is from central and eastern Mediterranean countries. Known as the dragon arum, it flowers in early summer, with a huge deep maroon-purple

spathe surrounding the dark spadix containing the true flowers. Its size and colour make this an interesting plant, but it also emits a revolting smell! Height 90cm (3ft).

Eucharis amazonica The Amazon lily, from South America, is best grown in a container if placed outdoors, and brought into a heated greenhouse or conservatory for the winter. The fragrant white flowers, borne in autumn, resemble short-cupped daffodils. Height 45–60cm (1½–2ft).

Gloriosa superba This is a breathtakingly beautiful plant from tropical Africa and Asia, with exotic-looking flowers that have reflexed petals in a mixture of yellow and red – like leaping flames. Its common names include flame lily, glory lily, and climbing lily. It flowers in summer and is best grown in pots in a conservatory and taken

outside just before it flowers. The form usually grown is *G. superba* 'Rothschildiana', often sold as *G. rothschildiana*. Height 1.5–1.8m (5–6ft).

Gloxinia, see *Sinningia*

Hemerocallis **hybrids** The day lily is not often included in bulb books as it is usually sold by nurseries and garden centres like a herbaceous plant, and not bought from bulb companies. It is included here as it has rhizomes and because it is such a useful plant for a sunny herbaceous border, flowering almost all summer. There are many hybrids, mainly in shades of yellow, pink and red. Height 1–1.2m (3–4ft).

x *Hippistrellia* 'Red Beauty' This uncommon bulb is the result of crossing a hippeastrum with a spekelia. The glowing red flowers resemble a hippeastrum. Plant in a very sheltered part of the garden in mid-spring, or grow

in pots started off in the greenhouse. They should flower in summer. Height 30–45cm (1–1½ ft).

Homeria ochroleuca A South African plant with short-lived, cup-shaped yellow flowers that have spreading petals, but the flowers open in succession to provide a couple of weeks of bloom. Grow in well-drained soil in full sun, and lift the corms for the winter in areas where frosts occur. Height 60cm (2ft).

Hymenocallis x *festalis* Common names include spider lily and Peruvian daffodil: it resembles a white daffodil, with extra spidery petals. It is best grown as a conservatory pot plant, or grown in pots outdoors over summer and taken in for the winter. Height 60cm (2ft).

Incarvillea delavayi Sold as either corm-like roots or as growing plants. A native of Western China, the trumpet-

Liatris spicata

Sinningia

Tulbaghia violacea

Zephyranthes candida

like flowers appear in early summer, above a basal rosette of foliage. Pink is the normal colour, but there is also a white. Height 45cm (1½ ft).
Liatris spicata A native of the south-eastern United States. Sold as either corm-like roots by bulb companies, or as growing plants. The dense flower spikes normally have pinkish flowers, but they can range from white to violet according to variety. Height 60–75cm (2–2½ ft).
Moraea polystachya This South African corm, some-times called the butterfly iris, bears unusual three-petalled violet-blue flowers with orange markings in autumn. It needs a warm border and some winter protection. Height 75cm (2½ ft).
Polianthes tuberosa The tuberose is a Mexican bulb valued for its waxy white flowers and sweet, heady fragrance. Lift for the winter

where frosts are likely. Plant in a warm, sunny position. If planted outdoors, start off in pots in the warmth to give them a long growing season. Height 60–75cm (2–2½ ft).
Roscoea auriculata These strange-looking tuberous plants come from eastern Nepal and Sikkim. The bright purple flowers in autumn have the top petals forming a kind of hood, with the lower ones a lip. They like a moist soil, in sun or partial shade. Height 30cm (1ft).
Sinningia hybrids These are commonly sold under the name of gloxinia, and the tubers are widely offered in seed catalogues. The huge trumpet flowers, like upward-facing bells, are richly coloured in shades of blue, purple and red, often looking almost velvety. They make wonderful summer porch plants in all warm regions. Height 23cm (9in).

Sprekelia formosissima A lovely summer-flowering Mexican bulb best grown in a conservatory or greenhouse as a pot plant. The deep red flowers are composed of six petals, the upper three wide-spreading, the lower ones like a hanging lip. The leaves are almost evergreen in warm climates.
Height 30cm (12in).
Tropaeolum tuberosum A perennial climber with leaves like those of the annual nasturtium, but smaller, with small, spurred, orange-yellow flowers. Needs a lime-free soil, and winter protection, except in areas where frost is unlikely. Height 1.8m (6ft).
Tulbaghia violacea This South African plant with rhizomatous roots is not widely grown, but it is worth planting as its sprays of bright lilac, scented flowers bloom for a long period in summer. Height 30–45cm (1–1½ ft).

Vallota speciosa The Scarborough lily is a South African bulb that blooms for several weeks in midsummer. The scarlet-red, wide, funnel-shaped flowers are 8–10cm (3–4in) across, clustered at the top of a stout stem. It is half-hardy and makes a good house plant. Although this plant is now more correctly called *Cyrtanthus purpureus*, you are still most likely to find it listed as a vallota in catalogues. Height 30cm (1ft).
Zephyranthes candida This is one of the hardiest of these wind or zephyr flowers, originating from Argentina and Uruguay. It is suitable for the rock garden or for growing in pots in an alpine house, where it will provide beautiful late colour. The white, crocus-like flowers are usually produced in late summer or early autumn. Height 15cm (6in).

Index

Allium giganteum

Mixed lilies in shrub.

ACKNOWLEDGEMENTS
The publishers would like to thank
the following people for their help
in the production of this book: The
Royal Horticultural Society (Wisley
Garden, Surrey, and Rosemoor
Garden, Devon) and Fortescue
Garden Trust (The Garden House,
Devon). They would also like to
thank Peter McHoy for loaning the
pictures used on pages 1, 7, 10,
11bl, 16tr, 17, 20, 22, 23b, 26tl, 32,
33tr & tl, 35tr & br, 36t & b, 37c
& b, 38t & c, 39b, 40t & bl, 41, 42,
52tr & bl, 53, 54, 55br, 56, 57tl &
br, 60, 61 3rd & 4th, 62 2nd & 4th.
Additional photography by Marie
O'Hara on pages 49–50, 55 and 59.